# As I Was Saying

*poems by*

# Constance Wrzesniewski

*Finishing Line Press*
Georgetown, Kentucky

# As I Was Saying

*To my family,*

*Dr. Chris Bursk*
*&*
*Master Poetry Class*
*at Bucks County Community College*

Copyright © 2018 by Constance Wrzesniewski
ISBN 978-1-63534-588-9 First Edition
All rights reserved under International and Pan-American Copyright Conventions. No part of this book may be reproduced in any manner whatsoever without written permission from the publisher, except in the case of brief quotations embodied in critical articles and reviews.

## ACKNOWLEDGMENTS

I am grateful to the Master Class Spring Poetry Workshop led by Christopher Bursk for sharing the love of poetry and their generosity in critiquing the poems, a family of well-seasoned and talented poets who, in the end, have collectively shared in the process of composing this manuscript. Special thanks goes out to Dr. Bursk for his disciplined spirit of belief in the written word and his eagerness to share his talent and knowledge with his students. My gratitude is great to all who contributed to my love of poetry and the expression of it. I also extend my gratitude to *Gwynedd Mercy Literary Journal, The Griffin, Schuylkill Valley Journal (The Pink Typewriter),* and *l5th & Oxford Literary Journal.*


Publisher: Leah Maines
Editor: Christen Kincaid
Cover Art: Constance Wrzesniewski
Author Photo: Constance Wrzesniewski
Cover Design: Elizabeth Maines McCleavy

Printed in the USA on acid-free paper.
Order online: www.finishinglinepress.com

Author inquiries and mail orders:
Finishing Line Press
P. O. Box 1626
Georgetown, Kentucky 40324
U. S. A.

# Table of Contents

Whoville .................................................................................. 1
Platinum City ......................................................................... 3
Stairway to Nowhere ............................................................ 4
Music Box .............................................................................. 5
Hurdy-Gurdy Man ................................................................ 6
The Deviled Clam Man ........................................................ 7
The Milkman ......................................................................... 8
The Ragman .......................................................................... 9
Through The Back Window ............................................... 10
PTC Car #15's Night Music ............................................... 11
Blue Suede ........................................................................... 12
My Mother's ........................................................................ 13
My Father's ......................................................................... 14
There's No Tomorrow ........................................................ 15
Inside 4459 E. Thmpson St. ............................................... 16
My Mozart ........................................................................... 17
The Engine That Could ...................................................... 18
The Pink Typewriter ........................................................... 19
Morning Song ..................................................................... 20
Strauss Tone Poem ............................................................. 22
Rosewater Turkish Delight ................................................ 23
Joy of Visionary Living ...................................................... 25
Frangipani ........................................................................... 27
Miles To Go ......................................................................... 28
Backyard Ant Tree .............................................................. 29
March 20 .............................................................................. 30
Written in Stone ................................................................. 31
Planet Earth ........................................................................ 32
Teahouse Garden Verse ..................................................... 33
As I Was Saying .................................................................. 34

# WHOVILLE

"A person's a person no matter how small."

When the last speck of dust
on the motes in the air
floats past for the very last time,
the jig is up, the last penny spent,
take special notice.

Wiggle your ear,
squiggle and tuggle
pull on the lobe
clear out the wax
get rid of the buggle
listen up close
you might hear a struggle.

Hear with your eyes
see with your ears
use everything you've got
you have to see it for what it is.
Take stock of who you are
of what you are not.

Roll over and over
around in the clover
till your dizzy hits delight.
When the sparkling road
comes into sight,
race down to the end
to the magic door
open, step through
to the jelly bean shower
that washes away your blues—
sometimes,
even your pinks and greens.

Dig deep down inside of you
the digger the deeper
till you reach your tiny
speck of self at the very nearly end,
find out who you are
look for your inner who.
Then tell everyone that
matters in the least.

Yell it from the Eyeful Tower
Tell it to the Mayor,
the Grand Poobah
if you have to.

But, let me tell you a thing or two
After all, no matter how small
it's the whos that count
not the whys or even wherefives.

# PLATINUM CITY

"Welcome to Platinum City," said the sign
as the miniature train chugged past, up
the mountain wrapping itself around the bend
straining  away the last of the sun's dimming
rays dropping off from daylight, sagging into
dusk.

The streets of the tiny town, just
north of Midnight, are lined
with opals and pearls the size of peas,
street lamps streaming their shafts of light
from diamonds capping the tips of ivory
poles.

Crystalline waters churn inside
the rim of the caldera, a bubbling pot
filled with opaque jewels carved
from quartz suitably illuminated
by the surrounding star
light.

At the very summit there is a free fall drop
into nothingness, a fuzzy film of snow
swirling around the highest peak that juts
into the surrounding haze of sleep.
The Moonlight Express has arrived at
journey's end.

## STAIRWAY TO NOWHERE

It was on Speakeasy Street
about thirty or so paces
from the corner of Eleventh.

Ten steps down to the seamless
door, a knock was heard, a panel
slid noiselessly aside.  A pair

of narrowed eyes appeared
in the small square, a card
raised to the impending light.

Moishe opened the door a crack
in the dimly lit shadows behind.
Two chairs and a table waited

in each corner.  Kate, too, with a
mile wide smile, a clap on the back,
a bottle of Genever Gin and a

"hey suckers." The musicians
showed up later, so did the
cops, sometimes, a shrill whistle

resounding.  A button was
pressed in the back room,
and the scene revolved.

A living room faded into view.
The 300 pound doorkeeper
was good at his job.

Flannery's saloon was safe—
one more time.  Prohibition
be damned!

# MUSIC BOX

Once I walked with beauty
in the shadows of a dismal
afternoon.  The day was dim
and drizzly, the gloom much

too heavy to bear, until she
took my hand in hers and
through the fine mist, she
led me to a secret music box

where we sat together, side
by side, and allowed the
mysterious chords to wash
over us.  The madness of Mahler's

symphonies and Mozart's
prodigious piano concertos
streamed into us like the
afternoon rain washing away

the sadness.  Chopin's trills on
ivory keys danced in our hearts
and our heads as we basked in
the glow of the lyrical haze,

while the vibrance of Vivaldi's
violin worked magic with its
strings and Madame Butterfly
stepped in at the end to scatter

flower petals at our feet in a simply
soprano manner.  Lazily, we passed
the afternoon bathing ourselves
in the secrets of the music box.

## THE HURDY-GURDY MAN

He needed no one to announce
his arrival. His monkey did it
for him. Scurrying around the
mustachioed man in the red and

white striped shirt, black bow tie
and boater hat, the monkey was
not outdone in his red bell-boy
suit trimmed with gold piping.

There was no set day or hour
for his show time. Whenever
the spirit moved him, he showed
up and was a welcome sight.

A pleasant smile for anyone
who'd come to listen to his
music box grinding its handle
to entertain with sounds of gaiety.

The equally friendly monkey
would tip his red pillbox hat
at the end of each tune collecting
tips and hopping up to empty

them into the tin cup atop
the organ. The hurdy-gurdy
man cajoled and cranked as
he wandered down the street

with a broad grin, and a deep
bow in gratitude to anyone who
gave his sidekick a piece
of change, no matter how small.

## THE DEVILED CLAM MAN

Mr. Johnson strolled down our
street every Friday without fail—
clockwork, 6:00 PM.  Set your
watch by him.

Crisp white—head to toe,
Gatsby cap, trousers, long sleeves,
oxford shoes, his black face shiny
with sweat from lugging

his heavy white hot canister
brimful with hot clams for sale.  It
hung by a wide canvas strap
from sagging shoulders.

Gathered unceremoniously on the
front steps of houses up and down
the block, we waited patiently,
thrilled to his sing-song tune.

Nothing more than a hawker
with a nasal twang, he crooned,
rising and falling:  "Deviled Clams.
Get Your Deviled Clams Here."

## THE MILKMAN

The white Abbot's Dairy truck
with the brown cow on its side
panel and squeaky brakes
was our alarm on Saturday

mornings at 9:00 AM when the
weekly bills were paid. His
wake up song was simply:
"Milk," but he had style.

He wailed it out loud and
clear. "Ee-yilg!" went from
middle C to G in an elongated
swell. We didn't care—song

or no song- all we knew, was
he had ice cold chocolate milk
on that truck and mom would
buy us some if we were good.

## THE RAGMAN

He announced his arrival
sinister in tone,
a cranky sort.
But his horse beat him

to the punch with its
steady clip, clop, clip, clop
and the jingle of its harness
which gave way to the vision

about to unfold. A grizzly
old buzzard filthy with lice,
I think, scruffy beard,
milky eyes hooded by a dirty

woolen cap. We shrank in
fear at the sight of him seated
on his throne, whip in hand,
his carriage, a rickety green

wooden wagon, red spoke
wheels. The song he sang
made no sense at all. It might
have been a foreign language

for all we knew. And none of
us knew any better. Nor did we
really care. "Any old rags or
papers" started out in a high

sing-song pitch and faded into
a very low glissando. His spiel
sounded like a long slide down
a child's board. "Eddy audy ody

yo brorek" is what we heard.
His bedraggled mouth barely shut
before we dropped the rags
at the curb and ran.

## THROUGH THE BACK WINDOW

The gingko trees fan out across
Roosevelt Boulevard,
arching in the center
reaching, straining to touch
like hands, branch to branch.

They join in the center,
tunneling behind us as we
emerge into the breeze,
the leaves waving goodbye
in the rear view mirror.

They run away from us,
in reverse, fade, recede
into the distant horizon.

The mailman walks towards us
and behind us at the same time.
He hugs the pavement seeming
to struggle against gravity, tracing
the path he will follow back.

He rushes up the steps
in the terraced grass,
to stuff the mailbox
before the car turns
and all fades from sight.

He hurries, delivers the letters,
turns in his tracks, races down
to chase after the trees
corner after corner
until he vanishes.

## PTC CAR #15's NIGHT MUSIC

The brute
cared about
no one
nothing
rattling
bumping
barreling
down the street.

It screeched
teetered
rocked
side to side
scraped
iron to iron
wheels to track,
friction
sending
a spray of
hot sparks
into the night.

Its bell
clanged
a raucous note
from within
its dilapidated
army green
shell,
its solitary
bug-eyed
lamp
a thin beam
searching
in the night.

A one-of-a-kind
Virtuoso.

## BLUE SUEDE

The languid way he wore his hair,
The languid way he slung his hips,
The languid way he'd lounge, not sit,
The languid way he'd curl his lip,
The languid way his words would drip,
The languid way his eyes would gaze…

He sang as if he never cared.
He sang like no one ever dared.
He sang of rockabilly life.
He sang wild, crazy, mellow too.
He sang direct, he told the truth.
He sang the best way that he knew.

Never strayed from his southern roots.
Head to foot he'd shake and hoot
Shouting songs to screaming fans, who,
Never once stepped on his **SHOES**.

## MY MOTHER'S

favorites were Jeanette Mac Donald
and Nelson Eddy, singing the
*Indian Love Call* in *Rosemarie*.

The pair of them easily sent her
flying directly to Shangri La
with their trilling duets. A pushover

for romance, she was sitting
in the middle of the third row
of the Edgemont Theater

engrossed in the operetta
when cousin Laura noiselessly dashed
down the thickly padded aisle

on tip toes excusing herself halfway
through the crowded row of seats
and leaning down to whisper

in her ear, "You have a gentleman
caller waiting for you at home
in the parlor."

## MY FATHER'S

taste in music was remarkably
well rendered. Long hair music
was not his style. He never enjoyed

an operatic aria. To his mind, it
was some poor guy yodeling,
or a diva squealing like a

stuck pig. What enamored him
most was a good healthy march,
preferably by John Phillip Sousa,

a man's man. Needless to say,
each and every Memorial Day
promptly at 9:00 am, he stationed

himself at the foot of the stairs,
apropos of an alarm clock, holding
on to the newel post and hollering

up to us kids to *make it snappy,
or we'd miss the parade* which
convened across the street from us.

No, Sousa did not march along,
but every school band in town did
and that made his day.

## THERE'S NO TOMORROW
*For Mario Lanza (1921 - 1959)*

He was a kid from South Philly.
Christian Street.  Near the Italian
Market.  At sixteen he started schoolin'
his voice.

It boomed out loud and clear.
Hit hard.  A cannon in the
dark.  Just like Caruso.
Only better.

Magnificent.  A romantic tenor full
of fire—a devil with the pipes of
an angel.  Every word he sang
was distinct.

He owned it.  And he felt it in that
barrel chest of his.  He made you
stop and listen.  He smashed it
home like there was no tomorrow.

He really packed it in.

## INSIDE 4459 E. THOMPSON ST.

The roll top desk in our basement
was a road map which led me into
a panorama of the past. Its smooth
dark hickory grain worn to a patina,

spoke of cavalier elbows, arms, fingers
that rubbed across its surface. I often
wonder, to this day, whose hand
splattered the indelible black India

ink blotch in the middle beneath the
secret compartment where I kept
hidden my 1943 zinc penny, my
sapphire blue silk hair ribbon,
my Gene Autry Dixie Cup lid.

## MY MOZART

Though she toiled away
at stretching her lungs
as a baby, my daughter
as an instrument, was something
I never deemed possible.

She abandoned her voice
in later years and replaced
it, wisely I thought, with
the keys of the piano
naming Mozart as her
mentor.

Her fingers flew over the
black and white sharps
and flats during practice,
never any attention being
paid to the count of the
notes,

much to the dismay of her
teacher who felt it was of
utmost importance to steady
the beat which, she, to this
day, labors at avoiding,
arbitrarily.

Instead, enumerating her blessings,
she places melody above order
in metered atypical Type "A" fashion,
playing with the greatest delicacy
power and energy, a symphony
in speed.

Wolfgang would be proud too.

## THE ENGINE THAT COULD

The principal's bench outside that office was
an old wooden church pew salvaged from the
junk yard.  *How fitting*, I thought.  *A temporary
parking spot for well meaning parents.*

On an improbable occasion or two, I found
myself there pondering life's challenges,
waiting my turn for a face to face interrogation.

*I think I can, I think I can,* I thought,
apropos of the little engine and its uphill climb.

Years Later . . .

A feeling,
decidedly of déjà vu,
swept through my body while listening
intently to "Pomp & Circumstance"
on Graduation Day
at Delaware Valley University.
The familiarity felt right, the hard seat
a comfort.  When the horns blared and my son
stepped up to accept his diploma,
he turned to the audience and flashed.
Fully clothed beneath his gown,
the T-Shirt read:
*Thanks, Mom and Dad.*

*I always knew we could*, I thought.

## THE PINK TYPEWRITER
*For Pam*

I dreamed one day of a typewriter
that needed no fingers to strike its keys.

It came alive at night and typed
throughout my slumber with no

outside help of any kind to make it
sing its staccato song and ring its

bell at the end of each line. The carriage
was pink with keyboard to match,

ASDF and ;LKJ were at home with that,
happy to roll out their tune in harmony,

in rhythm with the bouncing letters
that mysteriously appeared on the

white sheet wrapped around the
rubber roller. It tapped and sang

throughout my dream. Come
morning, it succumbed to daylight.

The keys went silent—so much life
inside, waiting to get out.

## MORNING SONG
*For Bob*

Every day, to be precise,
    at 6:30 I arrive at the
        kitchen window, my backyard
            alive with song.

The deer feed noiselessly,
    on crabapples, leftovers that
        lie beneath the brittle branches
            of last year's produce.

A few stray squirrels,
    skate across the frozen
        snow near the bird
            feeder already in tune.

The finches twitter
    and trill in between bursts
        of whistles and gurgles
            of the brilliant red cardinals.

The blue jay boldly mimics
    the raptor's raspy scream that
        roosts in the gnarled mulberry
            tree at the edge of the woods.

Spotting the danger that lurks on the perch,
    in full view of his prey, his breakfast
        before him, the jay wheedles
            a warning to his friends.

Downy woodpeckers, metronomes of the orchestra,
    drum a steady beat, behind the twitters
        and chatter of the starlings.  The trilling
            sparrows stand humbly in their shadow.

The hawk, daring acrobat, appears,
        a blur of motion, flurry of feathers.  He stabs
                the air, glides, dives, darts, an arrow amidst
                        the thrumming vibrato intermittently feasting.

Narrowly missing the deep throated jay,
        whose black necklace bobs in cadence with his notes,
                he circles above the tangled holly bush where the
                        ground feeders have frantically hurried to safety.

The morning song ends abruptly.
        The hungry hawk retreats, takes wing
                already planning his next attack.
                        The others flee quickly into the woods.

I smile to myself and leave the window to start my day.

## STRAUSS TONE POEM

Thunder rumbles
Rain splashes
Lightning crackles.

Running
Through the
Woods

Carried on mad
Wings of wind
Ascending.

Flung
beyond the trees
beyond fear.

At last
A golden shaft
plunges through
Ragged dark clouds.
It stabs, stabs, stabs.

## ROSEWATER TURKISH DELIGHT

Pistachios, rosewater,
lemon, sugar,
a sprinkle of cardamom's
zest.

The hatchet faced old lady
sells her
sophisticated confection to a melting
pot

of passersby at the Bazaar.
She sits
hunched in her stall beside the
goldsmith

listening to the dissonant
sounds of
the strolling minstrels who
pluck

their songs on the long necked
lute to
claps in sync with the drum
beats.

But the somber flute
captures her
melancholy, unmetered musical
poetry,

rhythmic jewels: Eyes half open, she
nods off,
Sees herself dancing to the twang of the
zither

in the sultan's palace.
Her gray
head bobs.   She stirs, clutches her
tambourine

beneath her black woolen shawl,
raises it
high above her gray head
·         Thwack! Thwack! Thwack!

## JOY OF VISIONARY LIVING

Bach's masterpiece, Jesu Joy of Man's Desiring,
    calming, soothing, methodical,
takes us back to another time, when life was simple,
    unquestioning.  But,
soon came Mozart speeding along in the next
    century with his spritely prodigious compositions.

Jules Verne, father of science fiction burst upon
    the scene with his ultra-innovative
ideas making his own kind of music
    catapulting mankind to new heights
creating his own Utopia using only that
    miracle instrument known as the mind,
his imagination, one century later.

Approaching the twentieth century, a young boy
    named Sikorsky
Watched a sci fi film about a ship propelled
    into the sky by rotor blades
His dream was born and carried with him until
    it came to realization.
Helicopters bubbled up into the air.

Was this the shape of things to come?
    When the Spruce Goose fizzled
and Ford's Edsel never got off the ground,
    We all wondered.
But then the futuristic cartoon, The Jetsons
    predicted the validity of robotics.

And, today medical engineering has the ability to grow
    body parts in 3-D
fine printing an ear in fifteen minutes.
    Potentially, the ability to transform humans
into androids through the power
    of cybernetics is now possible.

Frankly, I'm happy that my feet still hit the ground
            each morning, slowly but surely,
step by step, transporting me to my toothbrush
            at the bathroom sink.
That's music to my ears.

## FRANGIPANI

A canopy of creamy
        waxen clusters
                in the peak of youth

nestles in the dark
        of gnarled branches,
                their radiant luster

stark against the
        scaly bark of tree,
                their essence borne

on the tropical breeze.
        They flutter down softly
                in a gentle shower,

a fragrant offering to Buddha.
        An exotic serenity persists,
                saturates all Hawaii.

A powerful aphrodisiac,
        Frangipani's heady perfume
                is burned into my memory.

## MILES TO GO

Jazz is just like a cuppa hot
joe.  It flows down easy and
smooth.  Its warmth spreads
out like a mighty good booze.

It lingers in the memories of men
and their golden horns, flutes,
drums and the music they made,
guys like Louis Armstrong

who seasoned their pipes
with the raspy breath of
Dixieland's finest.  Its sacred
tones dug quietly into unwitting

souls, stomped wildly on the
hearts of the "cool man"
beats in fifties' coffee houses
eating up Kerouac's poetry.

It tore white hot into graphite
grooves of the music industry—
Cotton Club's Cab Calloway,
his "hi-de-hi-de-ho" scat,

ending up in vinyl recordings
of Pete Fountain's licorice stick,
and the blown out bee bop
of Miles Davis to name a few.

It's been stewin' and brewin'
for a mighty long time and
there's miles to go
before it sleeps—miles to go
before it sleeps.

## BACKYARD ANT TREE

Certainly
a hybrid
a late bloomer
last to flash its
wispy green shoots
along its scrubby bark

      Surely
      a remnant
      most undesirable
      oddly shaped one trunk
      upright the other elbowing out
      at a right angle close to verdant grass

Likely
A weed
grown wild unruly
tough strong resistant
to forces of nature we
dubbed this pinnacle of creation

      "Ant Tree"
      named for the
      huge black invaders
      that skitter along bare limbs
      while it drowses through spring's
      early pinks and whites outlasting the rest

## MARCH 20

Dark, cold, barren
earth explodes.

First responders
to nature's call
soldiers of spring struggle
crash through dirt's crust.

Beauty flaunts her victory
a command performance.

Flower bulbs incognito
bear multicolored garments.

Short lived they
blaze,
wither
cease
desist
too soon.

Late bloomers
salute the dead.

## WRITTEN IN STONE

If I had to choose a color for
my monochromatic surroundings
in that July heat of 2001 AD,
burnt sienna comes to mind.

Surrounded by royal tombs,
Tutankhamen's not the least of them,
I stood on a sweep of stones jabbing
into my sandals soles. Hardly a

luxurious feeling, I shuffled my feet,
glanced around. My eyes fell upon a
loose piece of cloth protruding from
the scatter. I bent down to retrieve it

shortly before our guide mentioned
casually it was off limits to confiscate
any of the precious antiquities which
flourished in our midst. Caught

unaware and flustered, I slipped,
with much reverence, the linen scrap
of mummy wrapping into my cotton
seersucker pants pocket and wiped

the sweat from my brow. It was written
in stone—I was a common criminal. I
kept it hidden and guarded for the rest
of the trip. Today it holds a place of honor.

Each time I open the door to wind
my steeple clock, I watch the pendulum
swing over and across the treasure that
lies beneath. I hold a weekly audience

with my regal fabric and wonder
which king buried in that sacred
valley once nestled in its comfort
prior to his fall from grace.

## PLANET EARTH

It's coming
It's coming
It's coming

Heaven's bells
continuously peal

Alert the young
Alert the old
Alert the world

Babies born on Earth Day
Mummies in Eyptian tombs

Space rocks
Asteroids
Gravity

A sudden burst of heat,
odor of sulphur, gunpowder

Will it be
Will it be
Will it be

Apophis
Itokawa
Andromeda

Rain of fire
Shower of rock

A collision course that will ring our planet like a bell!

# TEAHOUSE GARDEN VERSE

## ASIAN LILY

Wavelike basin lauds
        cinnabar Asian Lily,
                Abstract conclusion.

## CLEMATIS

Pale pink Clematis
        Cascades down slender raku,
                Star shaped flowers blush.

## WILLOW

Swaying in the breeze
        Slender leaves rustle in song,
                Willow paints the wind.

## CHRYSANTHEMUM

White Fuji Mum grows
        On rocky slope of hillside,
                Solitary theme.

## WILD ROSE

The scent of wild rose
        captures unsuspecting June,
                intoxicates it.

## TRIBUTE TO LI PO

Embracing the moon
        Death sips from your jade chalice,
                Life has few regrets.

## AS I WAS SAYING . . .

About my hall mirror,
it's the first thing you see
when you step through
the front door.

The gold frame is quite
graceful for all its fancy
curls, swirls and florets.

If you look a little closer,
run your hand over it, you
will know right away
it's from Europe, because

of the plaster on wood
composition which says
two things.  It dates back

to the late 1800's, and it
was hand built by a
craftsman. The gold leaf
came much later.

I applied that myself
from a small can of paint
once I rescued the empty

frame from the house where
I was born and grew up.
Before that, it was a
mawkish brown holding

a 3 by 4 foot portrait of my
maternal grandfather,
handlebar mustache front

and center, hair parted
down the middle. Debonair
you might say. Genteel,
by all means.

When I pass by, on my many
trips upstairs, I peer into the
reflecting glass and I still

see a kindly old gent who
once took me for walks
when I was little, stopping
briefly in the corner candy

store to buy me a penny bag
of pink wintergreen mints.
He's gone with me from

house to house on my many
moves—traveling companion,
dear friend.

Constance Wrzesniewski, a native Philadelphian, lives in Doylestown Bucks County, PA. She writes for the Bucks County Herald and has been published in several local magazines. Her poetry has appeared in *The Griffin*, the Gwynedd Mercy University Literary Journal, 15th & Oxford Literary Journal and the Schuylkill Valley Journal several times. She was a participant in *Making Magic: Beauty In Word And Image Exhibition* in the Michener Museum with both live and recorded readings scheduled to become a travelling exhibit. Her poetry collection *Watching Over My Shoulder* with Finishing Line Press has recently been published.

www.ingramcontent.com/pod-product-compliance
Lightning Source LLC
LaVergne TN
LVHW041552070426
835507LV00011B/1049